EASY PIANO

THE BEST OF ERIC CLAPTON

M000112095

This publication is not for sale in
the EC and/or Australia
or New Zealand.

HAL•LEONARD®
CORPORATION
7777 W. BLUEMOUND RD. P.O. BOX 13819 MILWAUKEE, WI 53213

ISBN 0-7935-2529-2

AFTER MIDNIGHT

Words and Music by
JOHN J. CALE

shout. _____
cream. _____

We're gon - na
We're gon - na

stim - u - late __ some ac - tion; __ we're gon - na get some sat - is - fac - tion.
cause talk and __ sus - pi - cion; __ we're gon - na give an ex - hi - bi - tion.

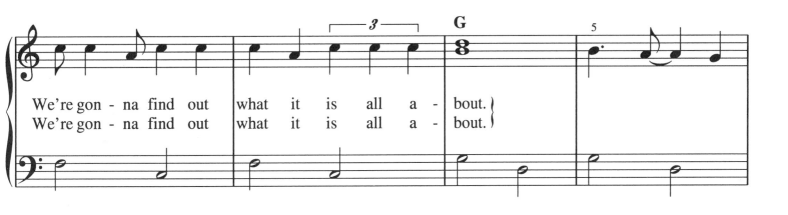

We're gon - na find out what it is all a - bout.
We're gon - na find out what it is all a - bout.

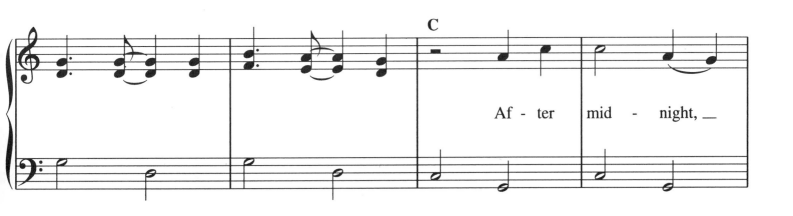

Af - ter mid - night, __

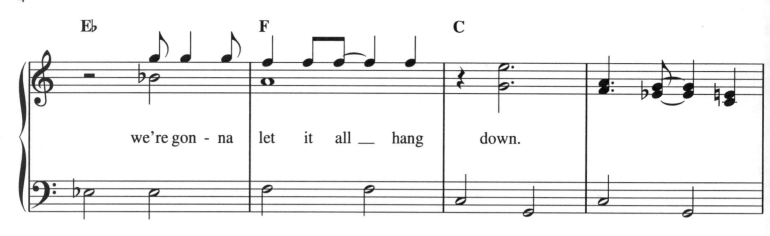

we're gon - na let it all __ hang down.

Af - ter mid - night, __

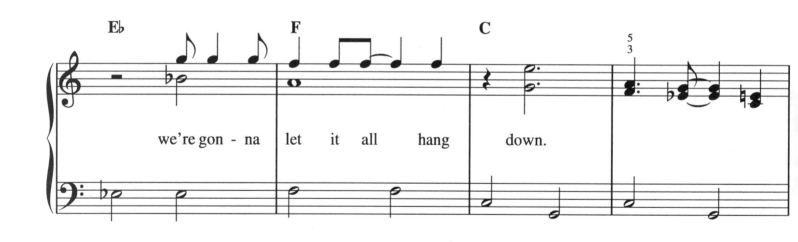

we're gon - na let it all hang down.

CAN'T FIND MY WAY HOME

Words and Music by
STEVE WINWOOD

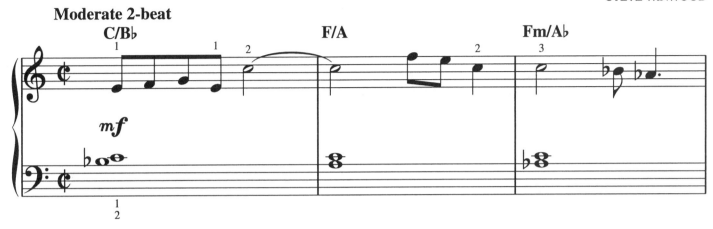

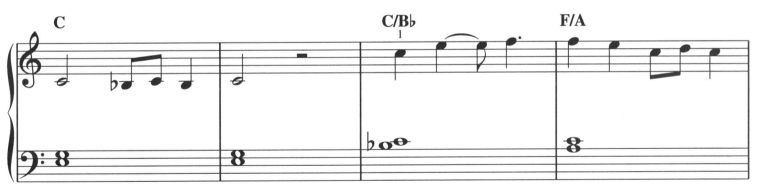

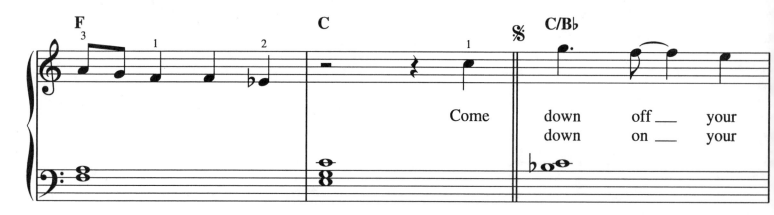

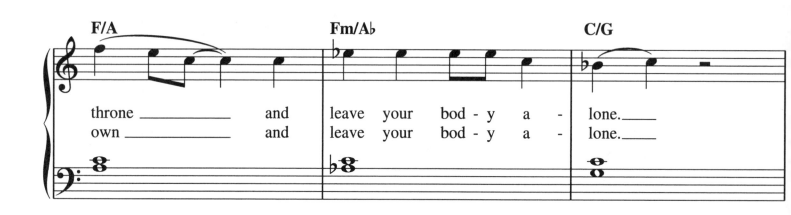

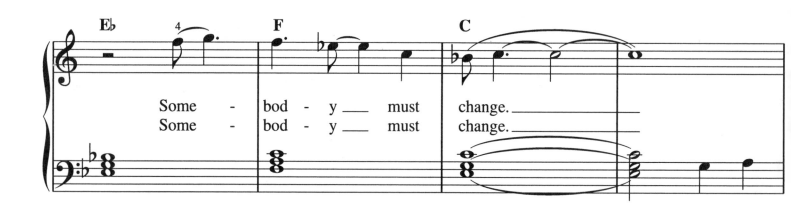

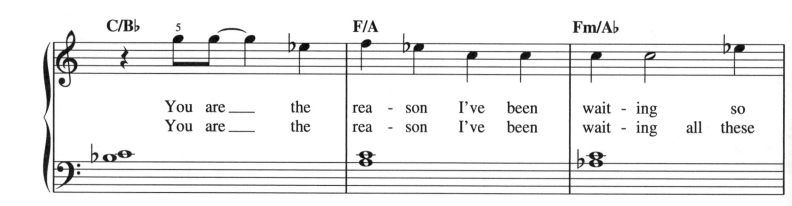

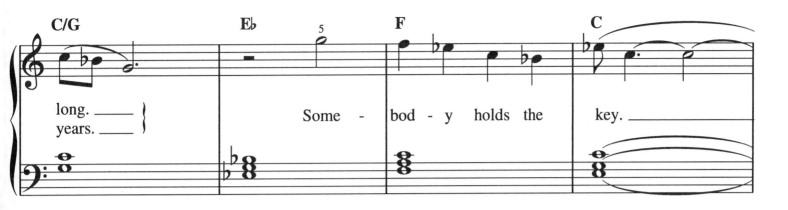

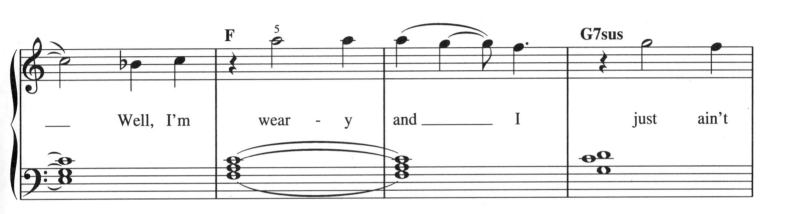

Come

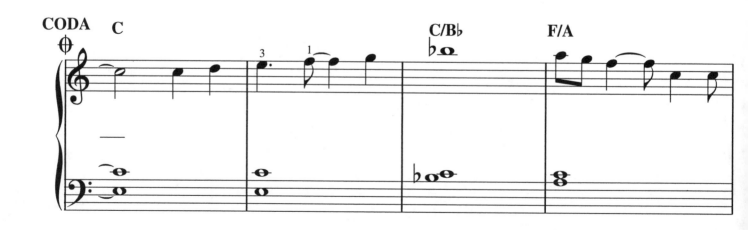

9

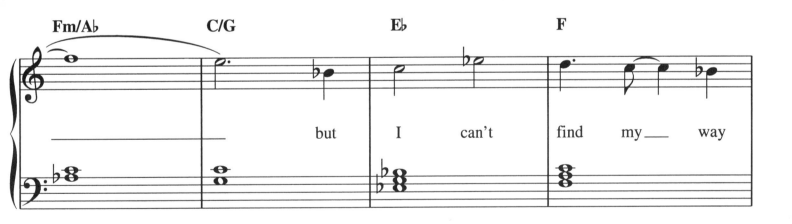

Ooh, _____

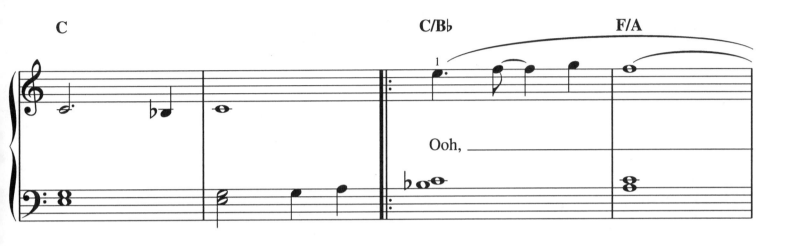

_____ but I can't find my ____ way

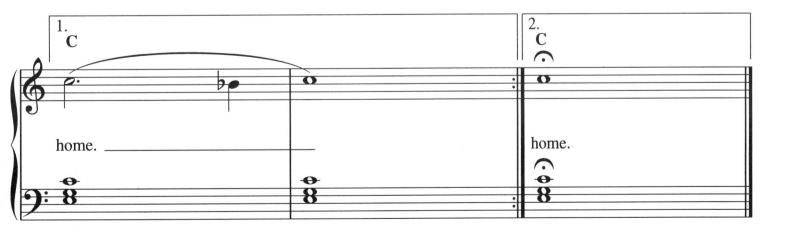

home. _____ home.

BEFORE YOU ACCUSE ME

Words and Music by
EUGENE McDANIELS

Be - fore you ac - cuse _ me,
Come on back home_ baby.

take a look at your -
Try my love one more

self.
time.

You say I'm
You know I don't

spend - in' my mon - ey on oth - er wom - en.
know when to fight

You're tak - in' mon - ey from some - one
I'm gon - na lose my

else.
mind.

COCAINE

Words and Music by
JOHN J. CALE

CROSSROADS

Words and Music by
ROBERT JOHNSON

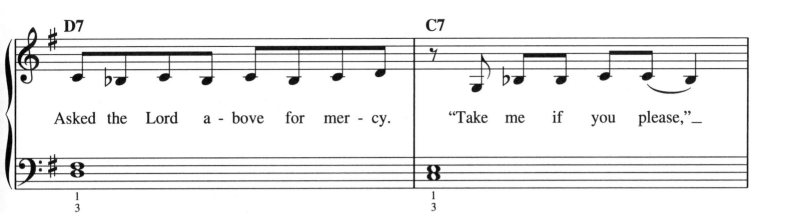

Asked the Lord a - bove for mer - cy.   "Take me if you please,"

1.,2.,3.

2. I went

4.

N.C.

G7

Additional Lyrics

2. I went down to the crossroad, tried to flag a ride.
   Down to the crossroad, tried to flag a ride.
   Nobody seemed to know me. Everybody passed me by.

3. When I'm goin' down to Rosedale, take my rider by my side.
   Goin' down to Rosedale, take my rider by my side.
   We can still barrelhouse, baby, on the riverside.

4. You can run, you can run. Tell my friend, boy, Willie Brown.
   Run, you can run. Tell my friend, boy, Willie Brown.
   And I'm standin' at the crossroad. Believe I'm sinkin' down.

DO WHAT YOU LIKE

Words and Music by
GINGER BAKER

FOR YOUR LOVE

Words and Music by
GRAHAM GOULDMAN

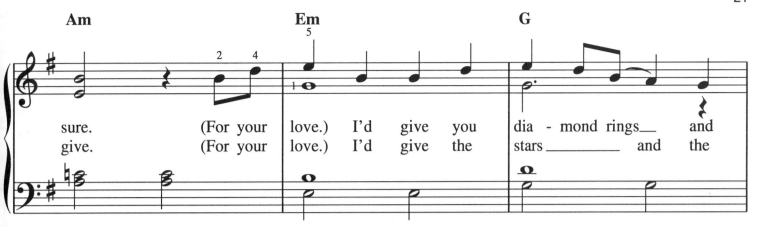

sure.   (For your | love.) I'd give you | dia - mond rings___ and
give.   (For your | love.) I'd give the | stars_____ and the

things right   to your | door.   (For your | love.) To   thrill you
sun_____ 'fore I | live.   (For your | love.)

with de - light. _ | I'd give you | dia - monds bright. _

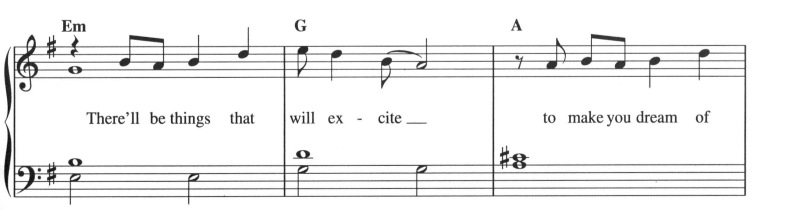

There'll be things that | will ex - cite _ | to make you dream of

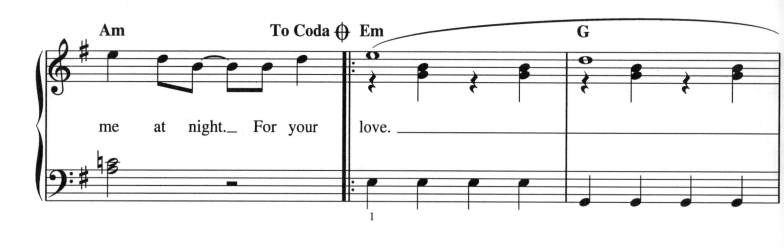

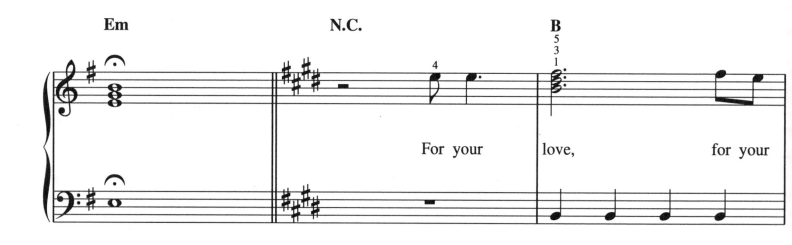

23

love, for your love I would give you all I

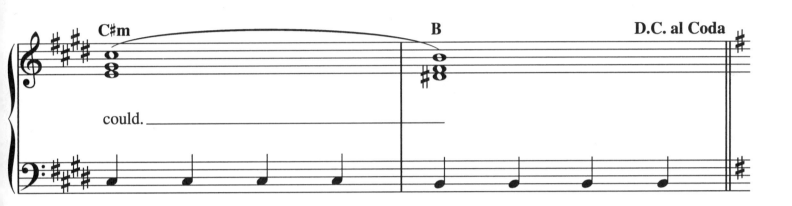

could. _____ D.C. al Coda

CODA love. _____

1.,2.,3. For your 4.

FOREVER MAN

Words and Music by
JERRY LYNN WILLIAMS

How man-y times must I ex-plain _____ my -

self 'fore I can talk to the

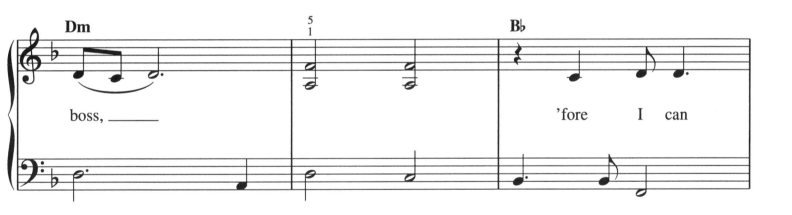

boss, _____ 'fore I can

talk to the boss? _____

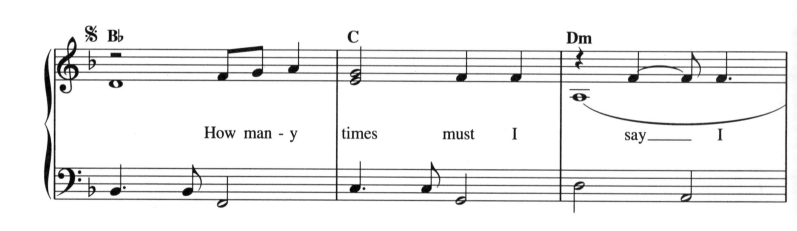

How man - y times must I say_____ I

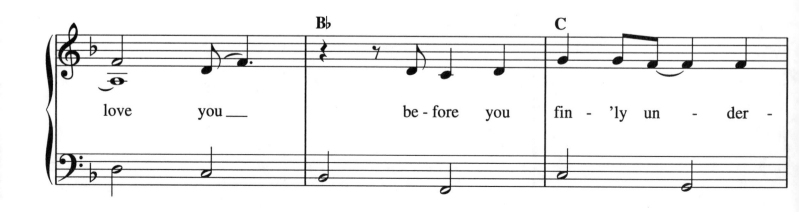

love you _____ be - fore you fin - 'ly un - der -

stand?_____ Won't you be ___ my

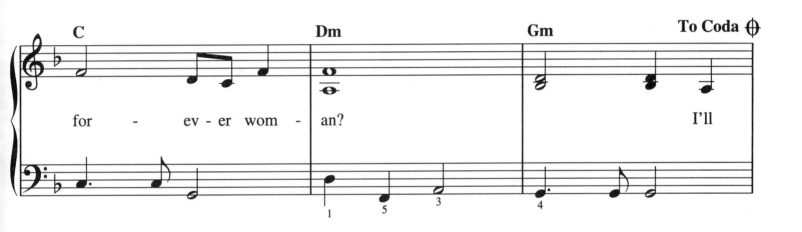

for - ev - er wom - an? I'll

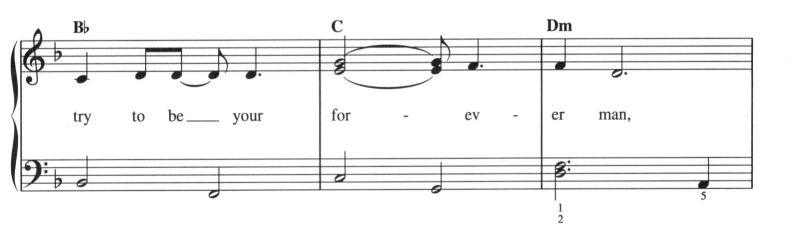

try to be ___ your for - ev - er man,

try to be ___ your for - ev - er

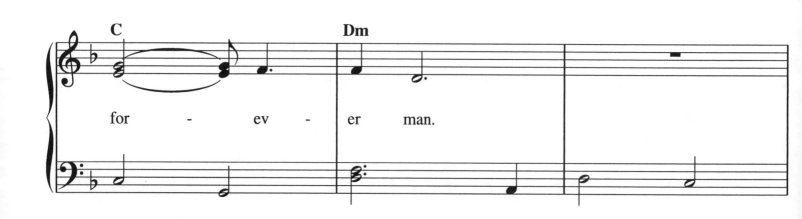

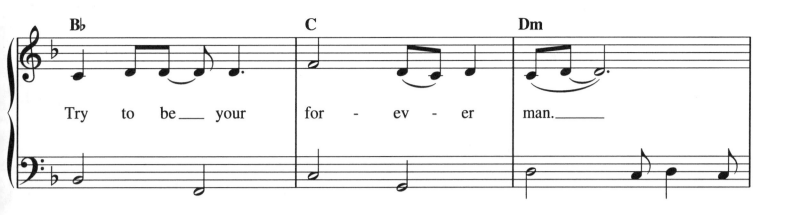

Try to be ___ your for - ev - er man. _____

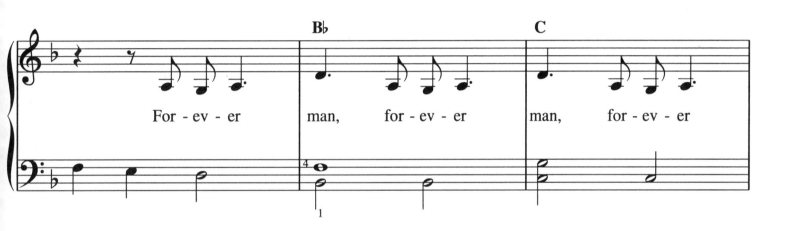

For - ev - er man, for - ev - er man, for - ev - er

man. For - ev - er man, for - ev - er

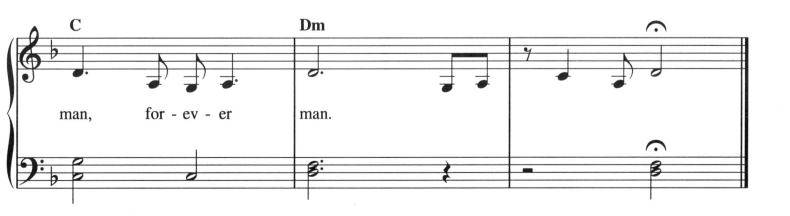

man, for - ev - er man.

HAVE YOU EVER LOVED A WOMAN

Words and Music by
BILLY MYLES

Additional Lyrics

2. But you just love that woman so much, it's a shame and a sin.
   You just love that woman so much, it's a shame and a sin.
   But all the time, you know she belongs to your very best friend.

3. Have you ever loved a woman, oh, you know you can't leave her alone?
   Have you ever loved a woman, yes, you know you can't leave her alone?
   Something deep inside of you won't let you wreck your best friend's home.

HELLO OLD FRIEND

Words and Music by
ERIC CLAPTON

Bm   **Am**   **C**   **G**   **D**

friend;   it's   real - ly good _ to   see you once a - gain.

C   **D**   **To Coda** ⊕

1.,2.

I
An

3.

D.S. al Coda

Hel - lo ___ old

CODA
⊕

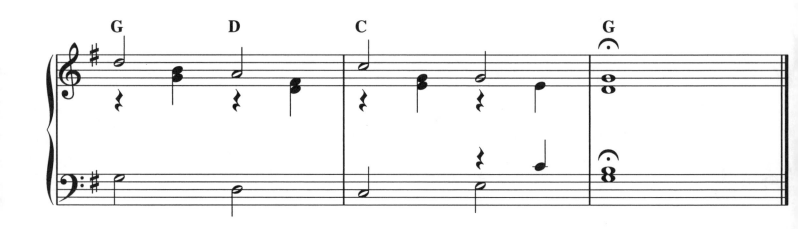

G   **D**   **C**   **G**

I CAN'T STAND IT

Words and Music by
ERIC CLAPTON

36

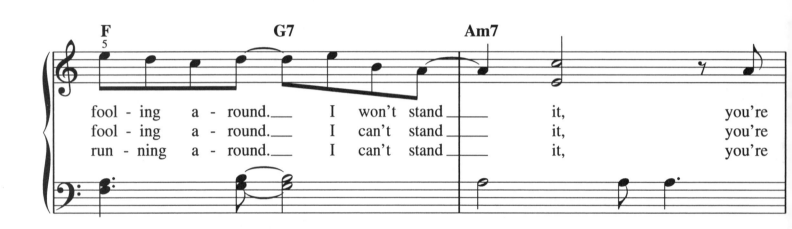

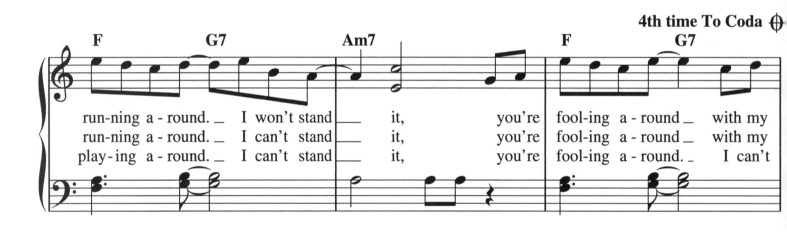

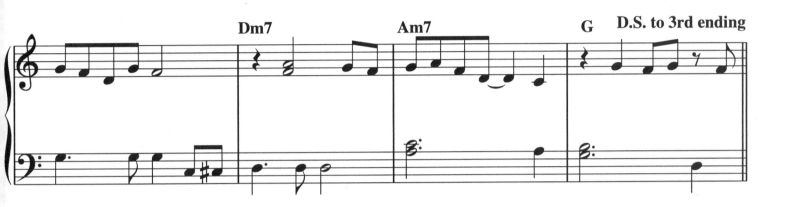

I SHOT THE SHERIFF

Words and Music by
BOB MARLEY

All a - round in my home town, they're

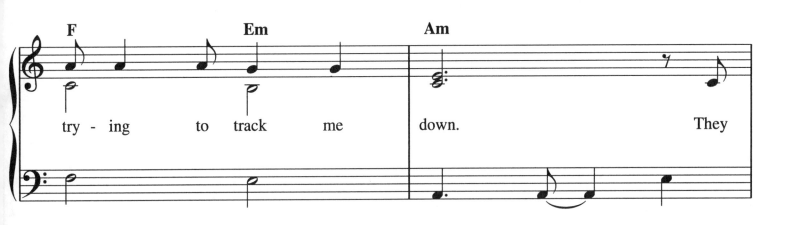

try - ing to track me down. They

say they want to bring me in guilt - y for the

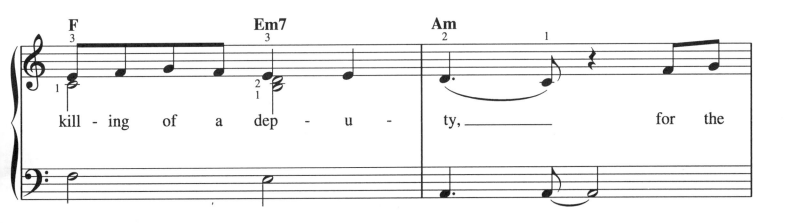

kill - ing of a dep - u - ty, _____ for the

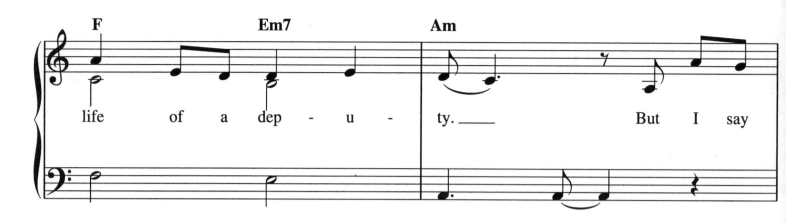

life   of   a   dep - u - ty. _____   But   I   say

Additional Lyrics

2. I shot the sheriff, but I swear it was in self-defense.
   I shot the sheriff, and they say it is a capital offense.
   Sheriff John Brown always hated me; for what, I don't know.
   Every time that I plant a seed, he said, "Kill it before it grows."
   He said, "Kill it before it grows." But I say:

3. I shot the sheriff, but I swear it was in self-defense.
   I shot the sheriff, but I swear it was in self-defense.
   Freedom came my way one day, and I started out of town.
   All of a sudden, I see sheriff John Brown aiming to shoot me down.
   So I shot, I shot him down. But I say:

4. I shot the sheriff, but I did not shoot the deputy.
   I shot the sheriff, but I did not shoot the deputy.
   Reflexes got the better of me, and what is to be must be.
   Every day, the bucket goes to the well, but one day the bottom will drop out.
   Yes, one day the bottom will drop out. But I say:

IT'S IN THE WAY THAT YOU USE IT

Words and Music by ERIC CLAPTON
and ROBBIE ROBERTSON

show.   Don't you ev - er a - buse___ it.

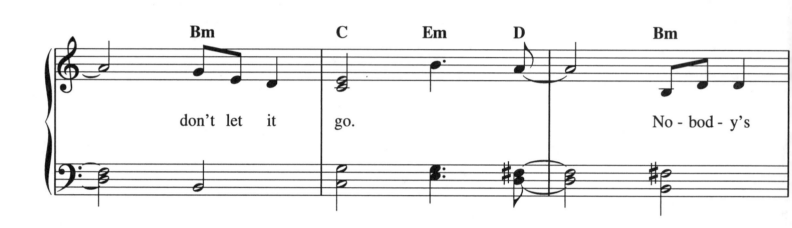

don't let it   go.   No - bod - y's

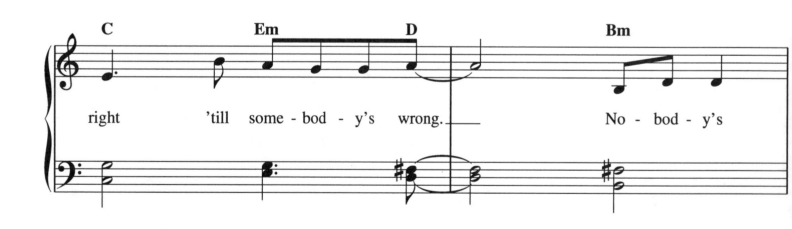

right   'till some - bod - y's wrong.___   No - bod - y's

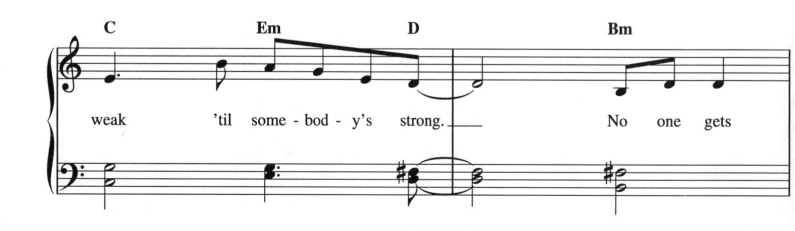

weak   'til some - bod - y's strong.___   No one gets

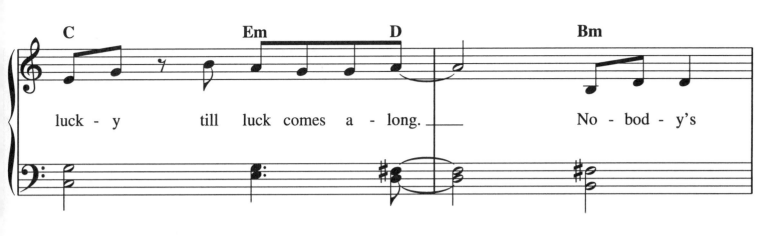

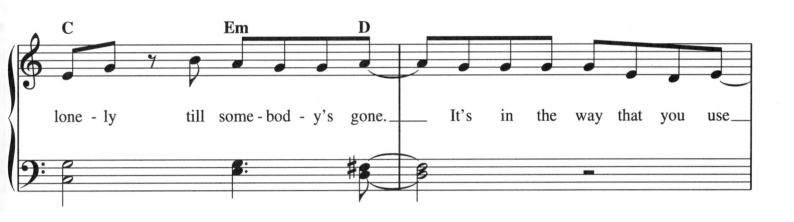

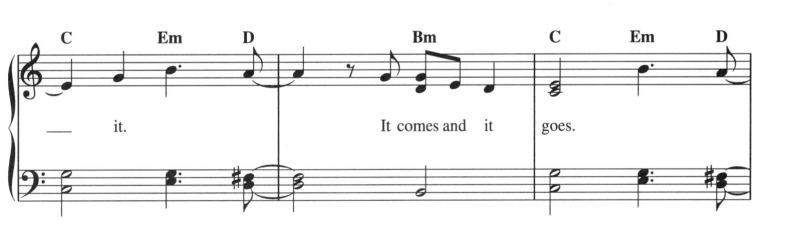

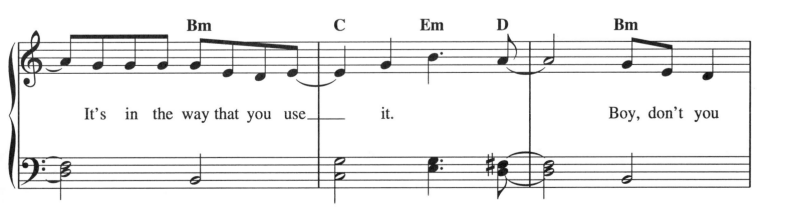

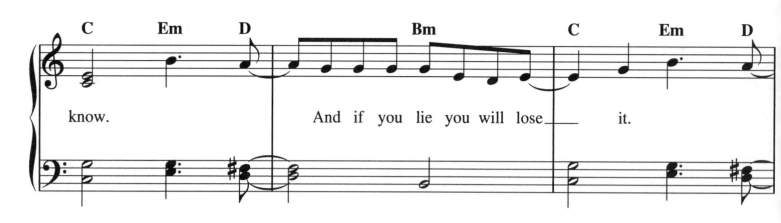

know.　　　　　　　　And if you lie you will lose___ it.

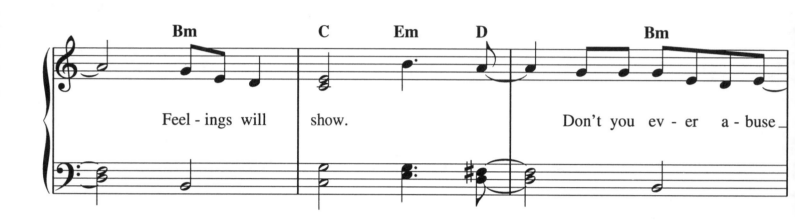

Feel - ings will　show.　　　　　　Don't you ev - er a - buse___

___ it.　　　　Don't let it　go.

I've seen　　dark skies but nev - er like this, ___　walked on some

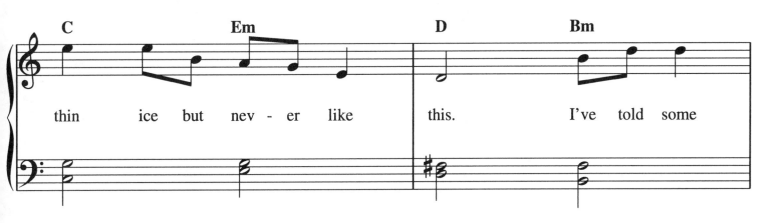

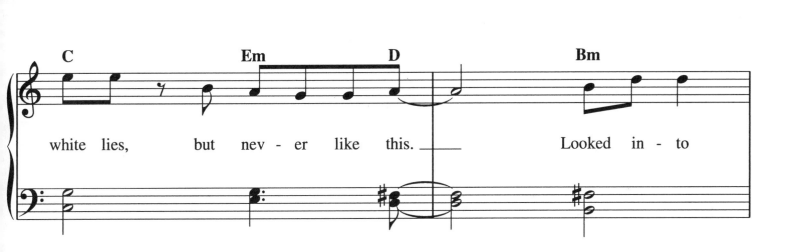

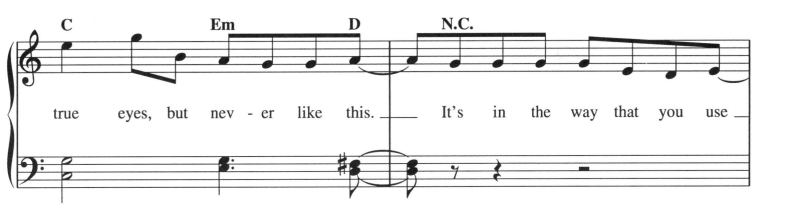

I'VE GOT A ROCK 'N' ROLL HEART

Words and Music by TROY SEALS,
EDDIE SETSER and STEVE DIAMOND

Moderate Rock Beat

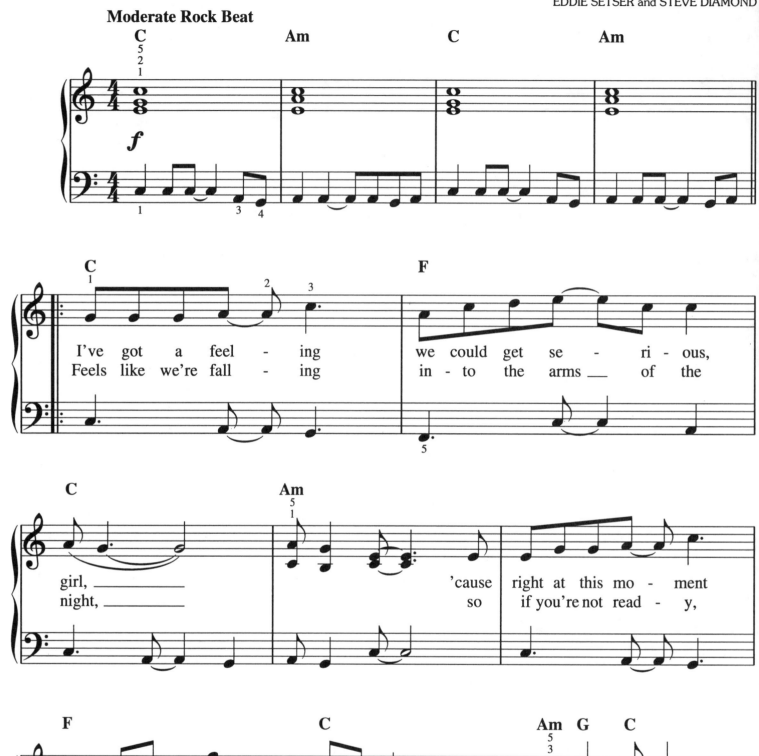

I've got a feel - ing   we could get se - ri - ous,
Feels like we're fall - ing   in - to the arms ___ of the

girl, _____   'cause   right at this mo - ment
night, _____   so   if you're not read - y,

I could prom-ise you the   world. ___
don't be hold-ing me so   tight. ___   Be -

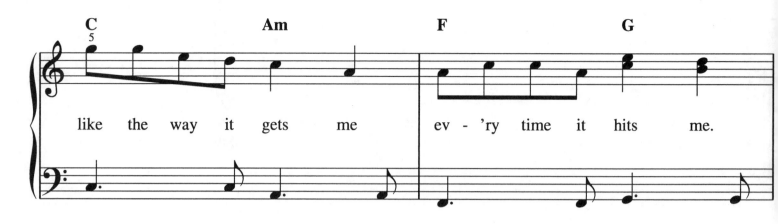

like the way it gets me ev - 'ry time it hits me.

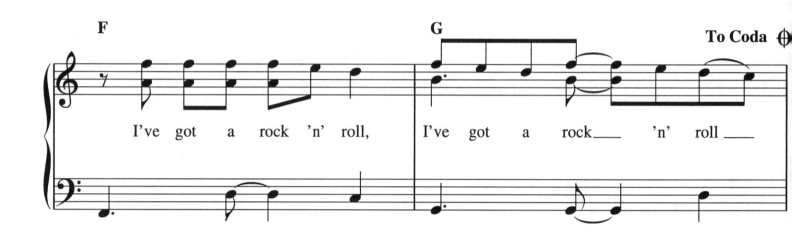

I've got a rock 'n' roll, I've got a rock___ 'n' roll ___

To Coda ⊕

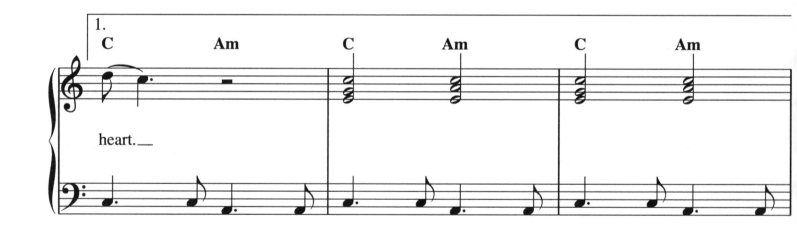

1.

heart.___

2.

heart.___

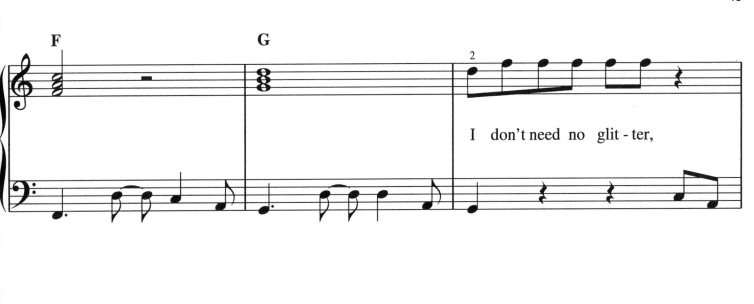

F

G

2

I don't need no glit - ter,

no Hol - ly - wood.

All you got to do   is   lay it down, and you

D.S. al Coda

lay   it down good.___

CODA

C

Am

heart.___

C

Am

C

Am

F

G7

C

I've got   you've got a   rock 'n' roll heart.___

LAY DOWN SALLY

Words and Music by ERIC CLAPTON,
MARCY LEVY and GEORGE TERRY

There is   noth - ing   that   is   wrong   in
sun   ain't   near - ly   on   the   rise,   and
long   to   see ___ the   morn - ing   rise   light

want - ing   you ___ to   stay   here ___ with   me.
we   still   got ___ the   moon   and   stars ___ a -   bove.
col - or - ing ___ your   face   so   dream - i - ly.

                    I   know   you've   got ___ some -
                    So   Un - der - neath   the
                               don't   you   go ___ and

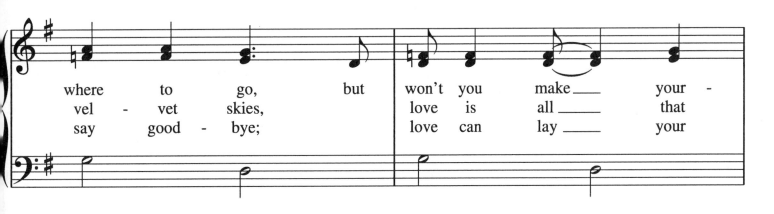

where to go, but won't you make ___ your -
vel - vet skies, love is all ___ that
say good - bye; love can lay ___ your

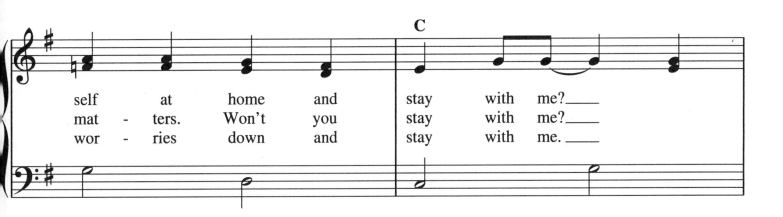

C

self at home and stay with me? ___
mat - ters. Won't you stay with me? ___
wor - ries down and stay with me. ___

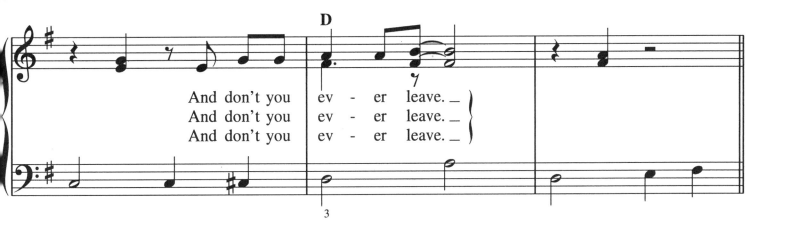

D

And don't you ev - er leave. _
And don't you ev - er leave. _
And don't you ev - er leave. _

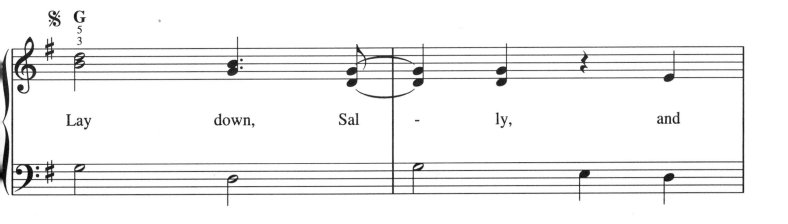

G

Lay down, Sal - ly, and

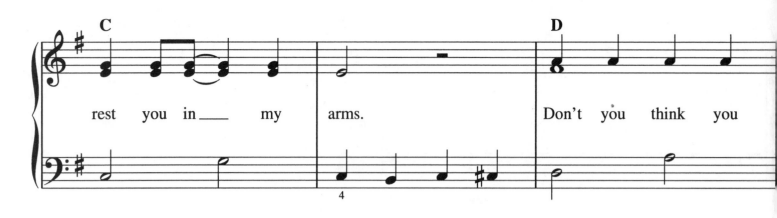

rest you in ___ my arms. Don't you think you

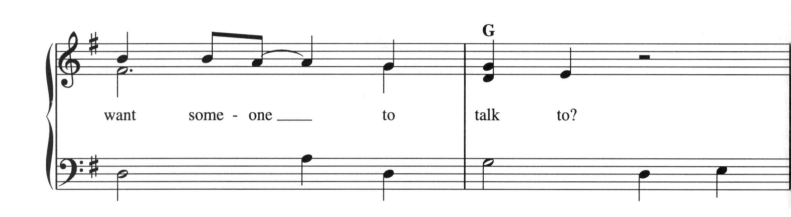

want some - one ___ to talk to?

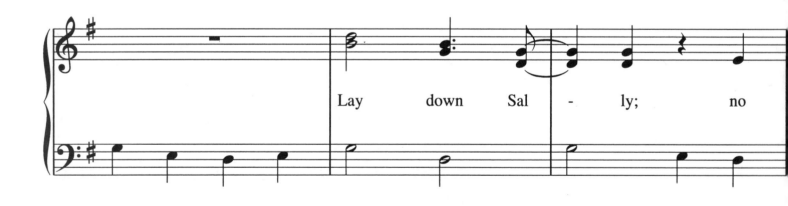

Lay down Sal - ly; no

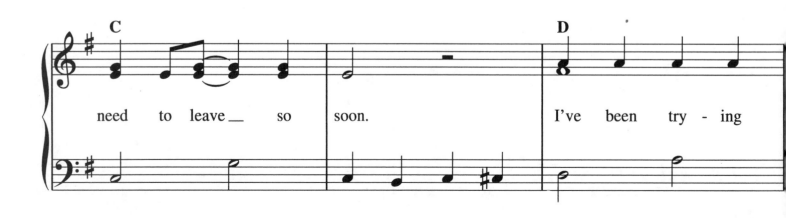

need to leave ___ so soon. I've been try - ing

53

LAYLA

Words and Music by
ERIC CLAPTON and JIM GORDON

dar-ling, won't you ease my wor-ried mind?

Lay - la,

CODA

Freely

dar - ling, won't you ease my wor - ried mind?

LET IT GROW

Words and Music by
ERIC CLAPTON

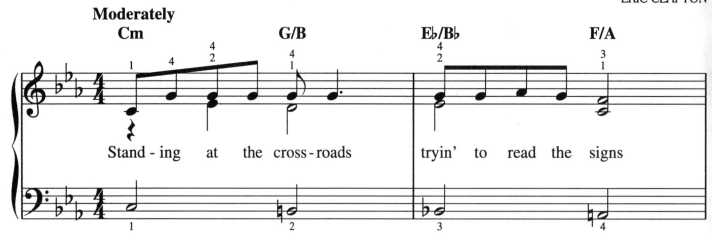

Stand - ing at the cross - roads tryin' to read the signs

to tell me which way I should go to find the an - swers and

all the time I know. plant your love and let it

grow. Let it grow, let it grow.

Let it blos - som, let it flow.

In the sun, the rain, the snow,

love is love - ly. Let it grow.

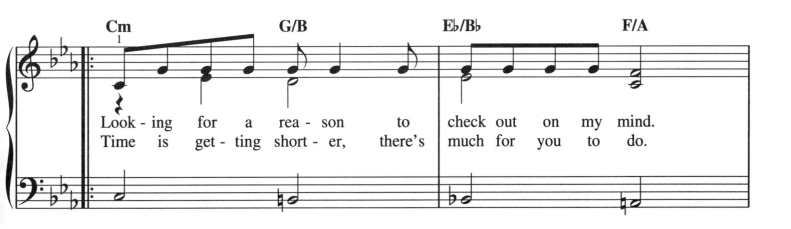

Look - ing for a rea - son to check out on my mind.
Time is get - ting short - er, there's much for you to do.

60

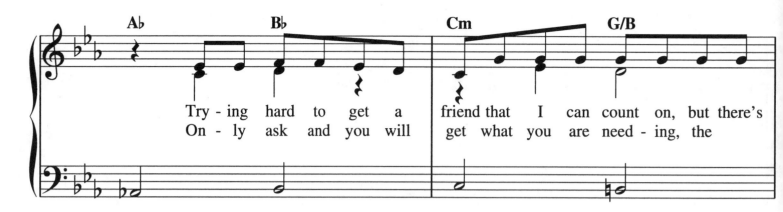

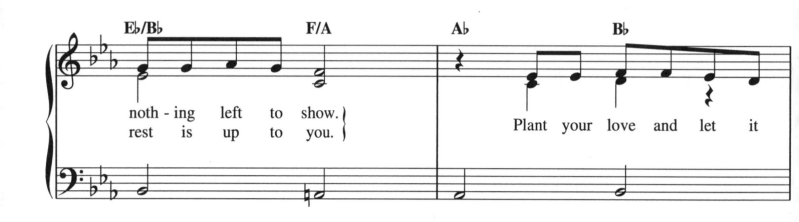

In the sun, the rain, the snow,

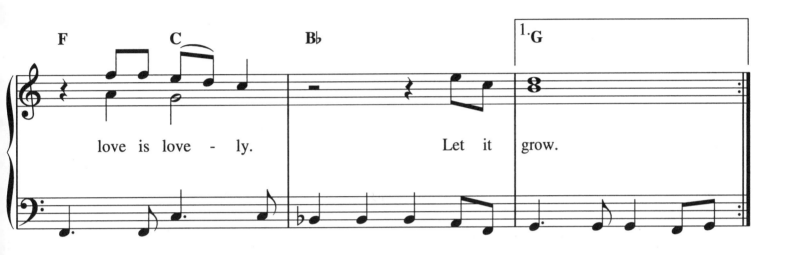

love is love - ly.

Let it grow.

grow.

LOVIN' YOU, LOVIN' ME

Words and Music by ERIC CLAPTON
and BONNIE BRAMLETT

Bright Country Beat

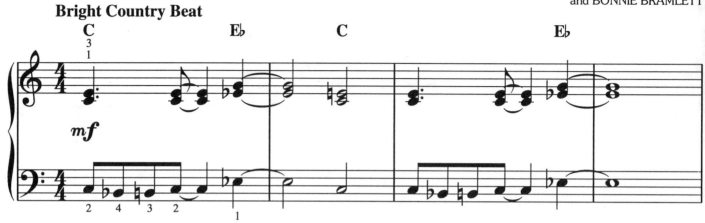

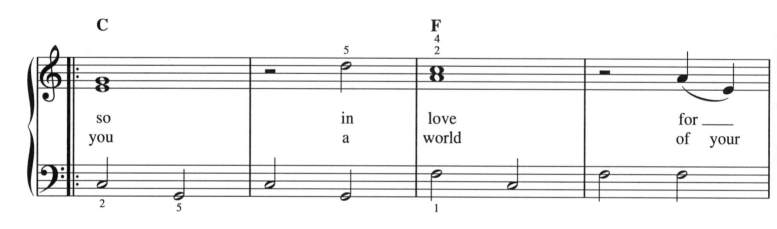

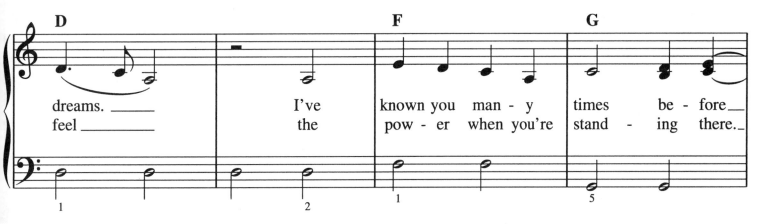

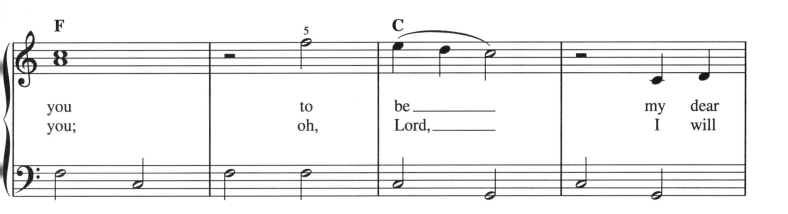

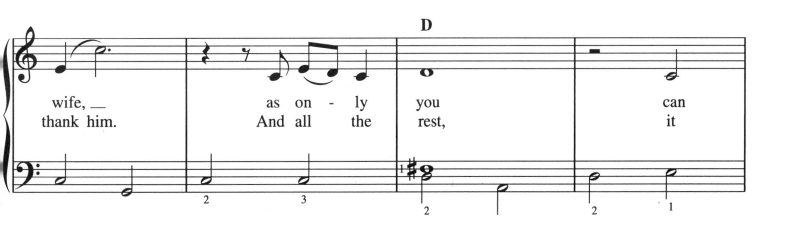

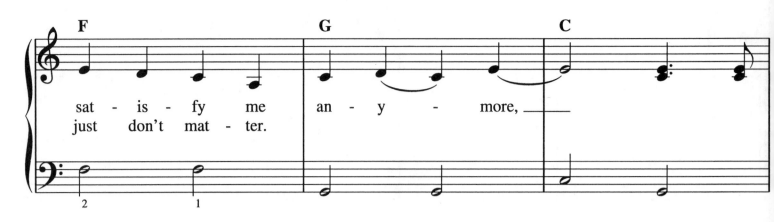

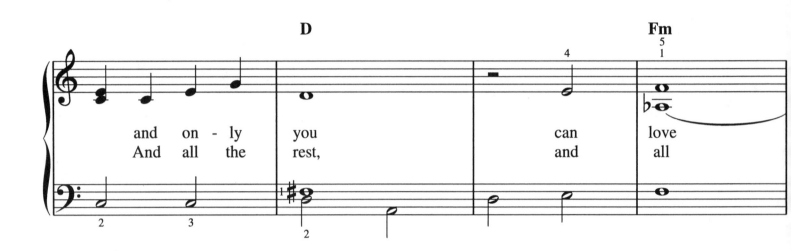

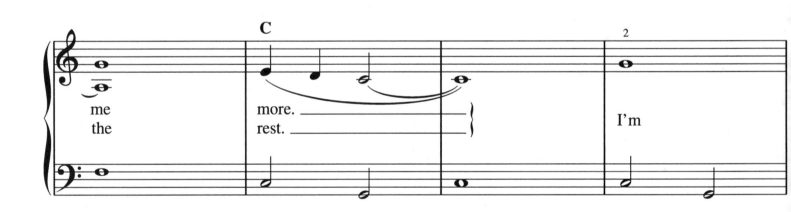

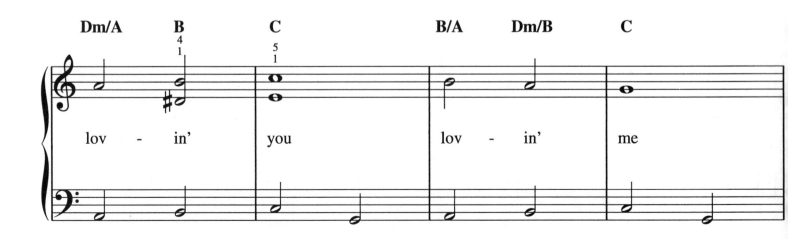

65

lov - in' you.   It's all the   same _____

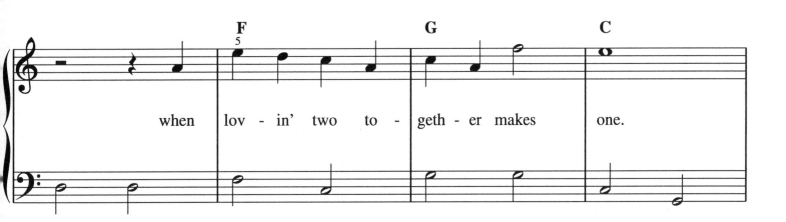

when lov - in' two to - geth - er makes   one.

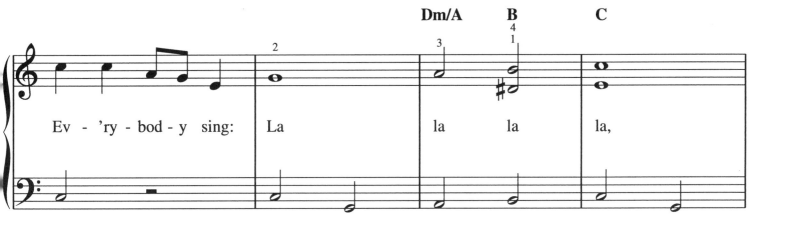

Ev - 'ry - bod - y sing: La   la   la   la,

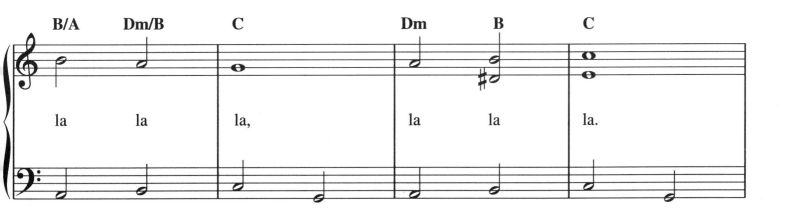

la   la   la,   la   la   la.

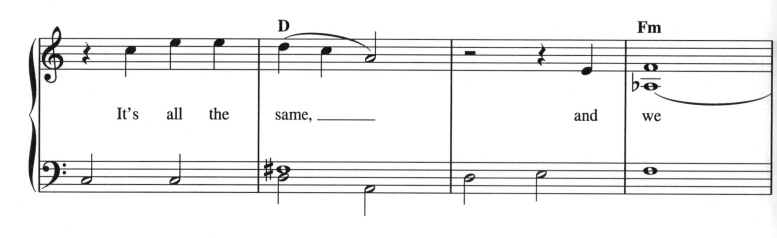

It's all the same, _____ and we

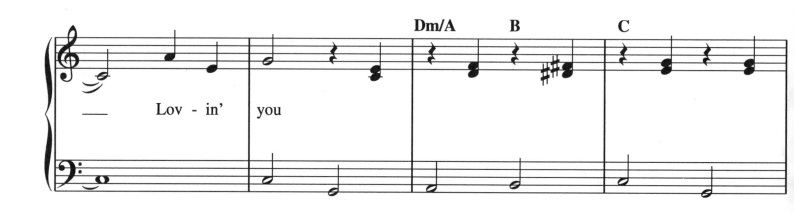

are one. _____ I will give one. _____

_____ Lov - in' you

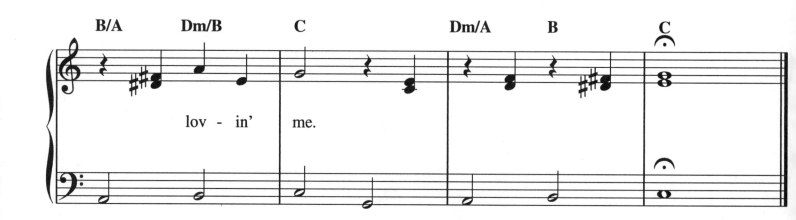

lov - in' me.

PROMISES

Words and Music by RICHARD FELDMAN
and ROGER LINN

Brisk Country Rock feel

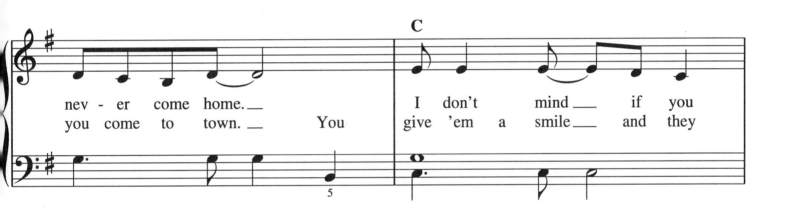

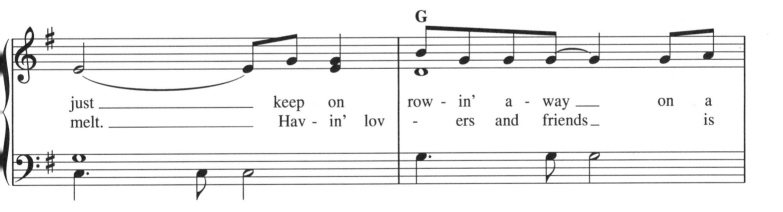

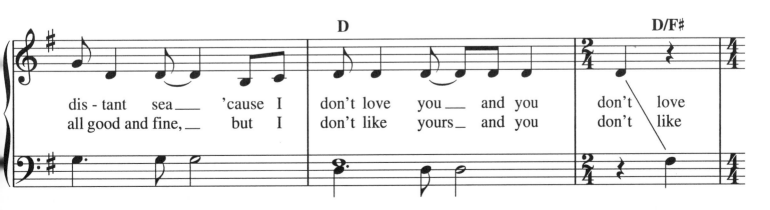

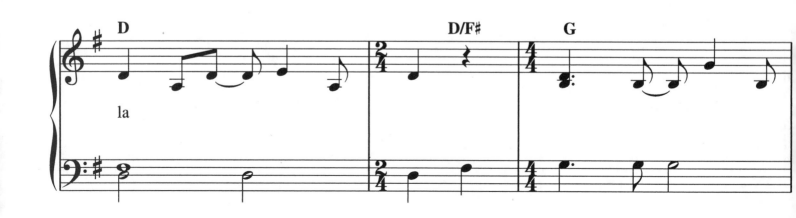

I don't care__ what you do at night __ oh, __ and
I tried to love _ you for years up - on years. You re-

I don't care __ how you get your de - lights. __ I'll __
fused to take __ me for real.

leave you a - lone. __ I'll __ just let it be. __ I
It's time you saw __ what I want you to see, and I'd

don't love you and you don't love me.
still love you if you'd just love me.

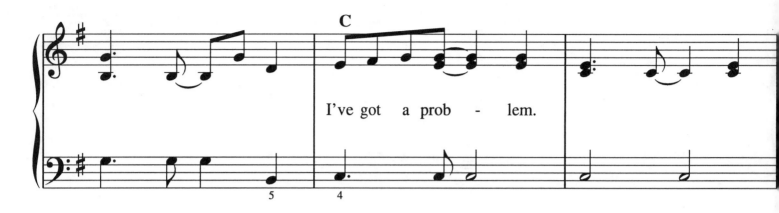

I've got a prob - lem.

Can you re - late?___   I got a wom - an

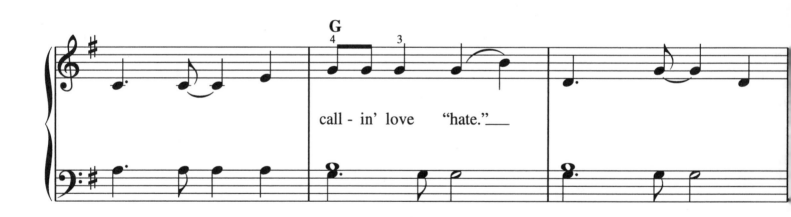

call - in' love "hate."___

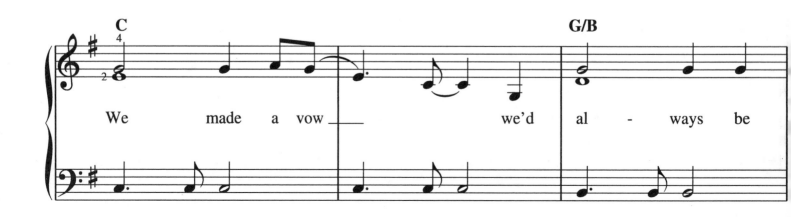

We made a vow ___   we'd   al - ways   be

friends. ___

How could we know that prom - is - es ___

___ end?

La la

la la la ___ la ___ la.

La la

la la la ___ la ___ la.

NOBODY KNOWS YOU
WHEN YOU'RE DOWN AND OUT

Words and Music by
JIMMIE COX

MCA music publishing

bought boot - leg whis - key. ____ cham-pagne and

wine. ____ Then I be - gan ____ to fall so

low. Lost all my good friends; __

I did not have no - where to go. I get my

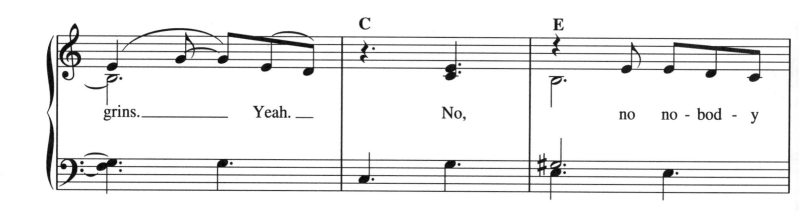

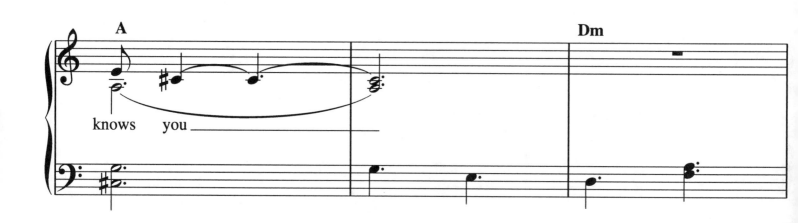

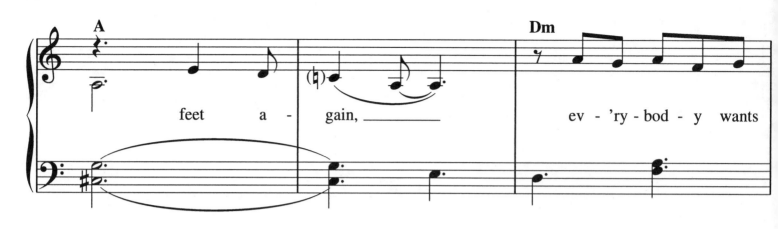

feet a - gain, _____ ev - 'ry - bod - y wants

to be _____ your long lost friend.

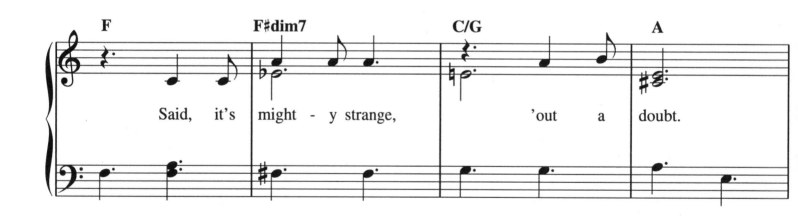

Said, it's might - y strange, 'out a doubt.

No - bod - y knows you, __

RUNNING ON FAITH

Words and Music by
JERRY WILLIAMS

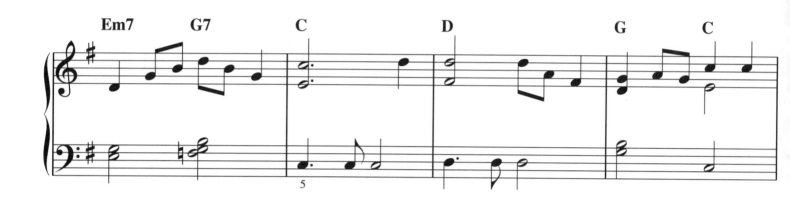

Late-ly, I've been run-nin' on faith.
Late-ly, I've been talk-in' in my sleep.

What else can a poor boy do? But my world will be right_ when
Can't im-ag-ine what I'd have to say 'cept my world will be right_ when

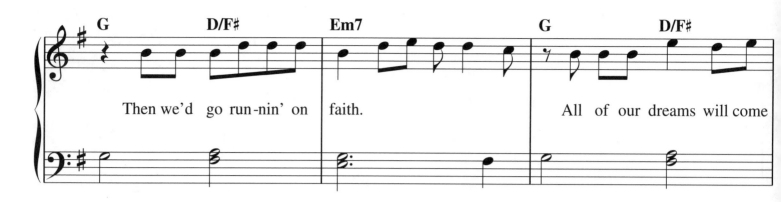

Then we'd go run-nin' on faith. All of our dreams will come

true, _____ and our world would be right_ when love comes o-ver me and

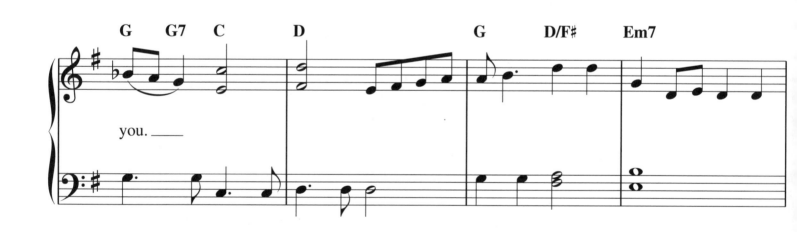

you. _____

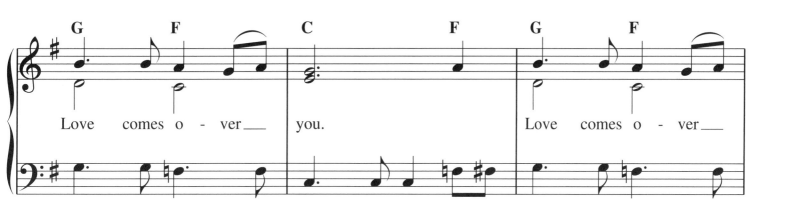

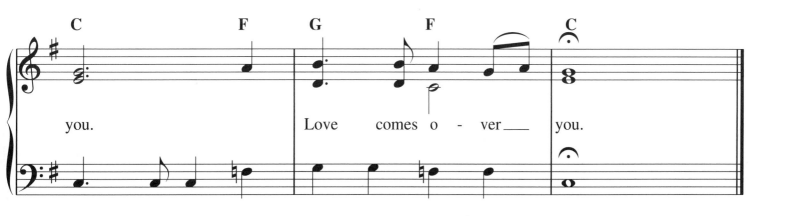

SEA OF JOY

Words and Music by
STEVE WINWOOD

Following the shadows of the skies,
Once the door swings open into space,
Instrumental
or are they only figments of my eyes?
and I'm already waiting in disguise.

And I'm | feel-ing close to | when __ the race __ is run.
Oh, | is it just a | thorn __ be-tween __ my eyes? __
Oh, | is it just a | thorn __ be-tween __ my eyes? __

Wait-ing in __ our | boats to __ set

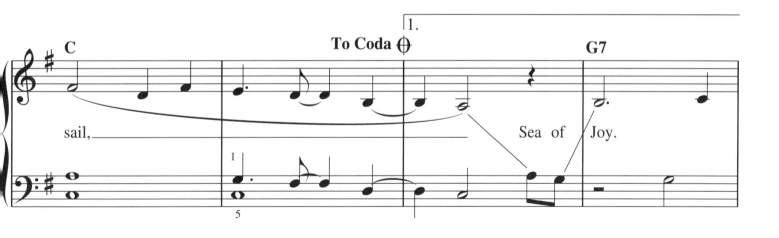

sail, _____ Sea of Joy.

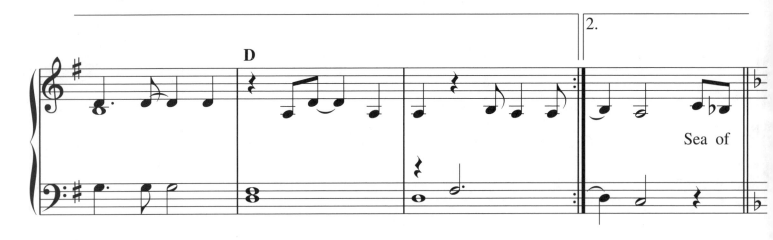

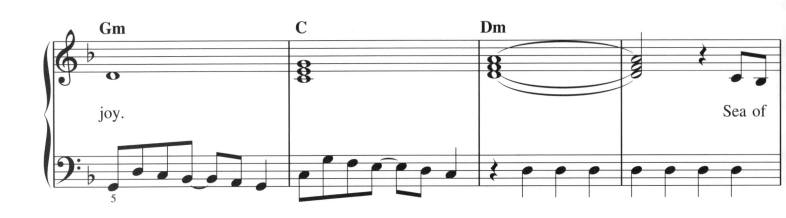

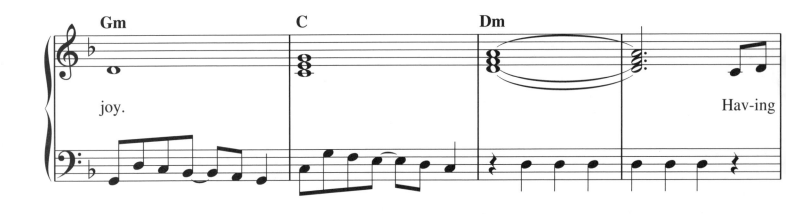

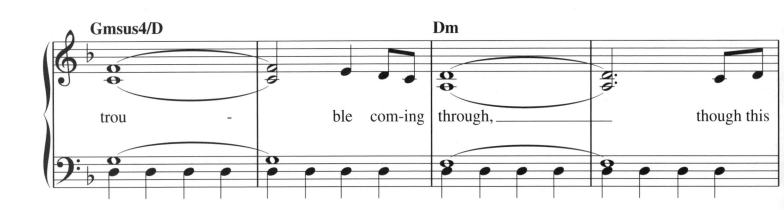

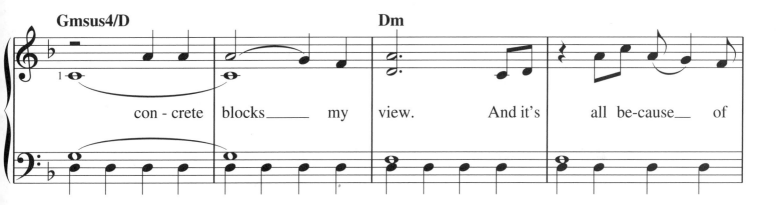

con - crete blocks_____ my view. And it's all be-cause___ of

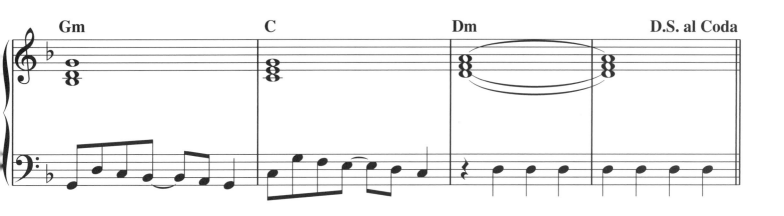

you.

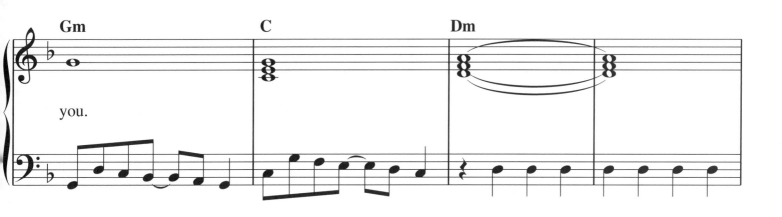

D.S. al Coda

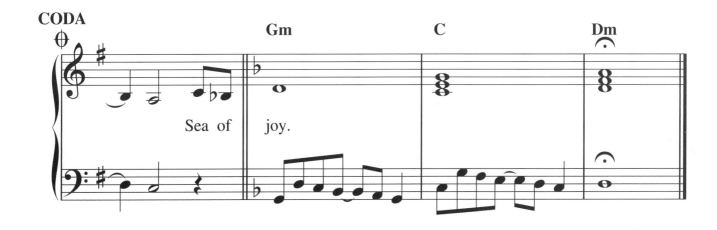

CODA

Sea of joy.

SIGNE

By ERIC CLAPTON

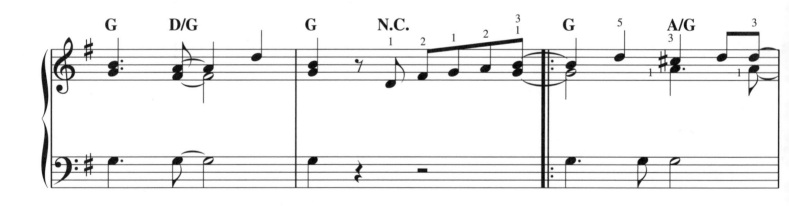

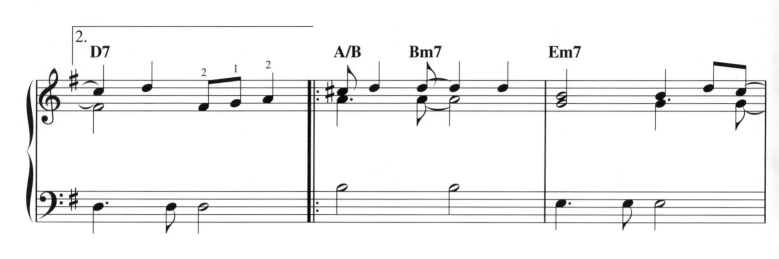

STRANGE BREW

Words and Music by ERIC CLAPTON,
FELIX PAPPALARDI and GAIL COLLINS

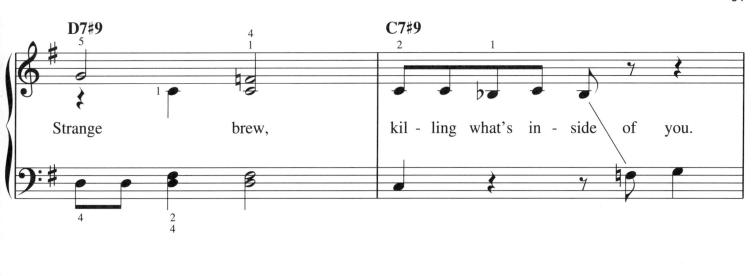

Strange brew, kil - ling what's in - side of you.

She's a

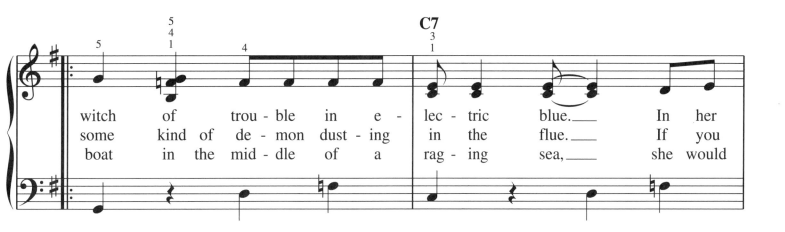

witch of trou - ble in e - lec - tric blue.____ In her
some kind of de - mon dust - ing in the flue.____ If you
boat in the mid - dle of a rag - ing sea,____ she would

own mad mind she's in love with you, with
don't watch out, it - 'll stick to you, to
make a scene for it all to be ig -

C7

you.
you.
nored.

Now what you gon - na do?
What kind of fool are you?
And would - n't you be bored?

G7

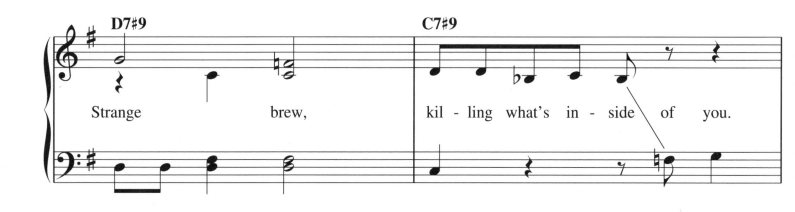

D7#9

C7#9

Strange   brew,   kil - ling what's in - side of you.

1.,2.

3.

G7

G7

She's
On a

THE SUNSHINE OF YOUR LOVE

Words and Music by JACK BRUCE,
PETE BROWN and ERIC CLAPTON

It's get-ting near dawn; when the
with you, my love;

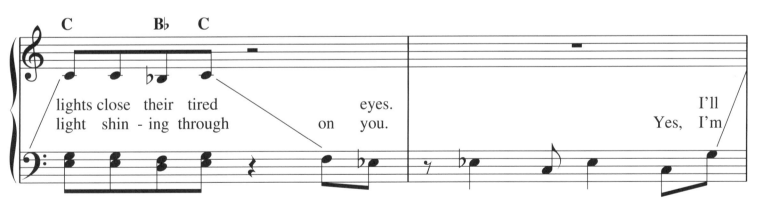

lights close their tired eyes. I'll
light shin - ing through on you. Yes, I'm

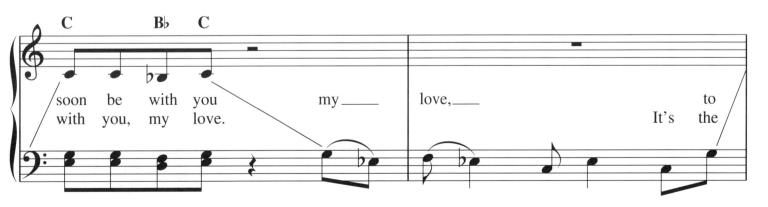

soon be with you my love, to
with you, my love. It's the

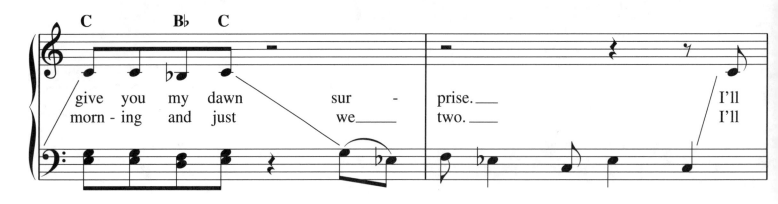

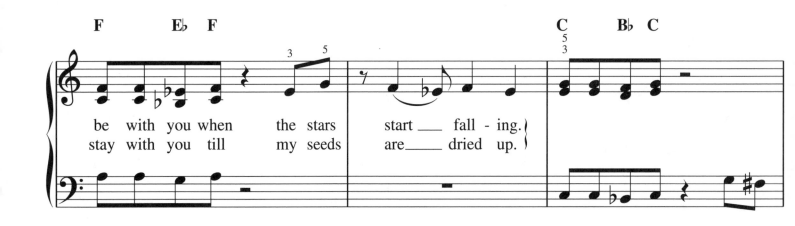

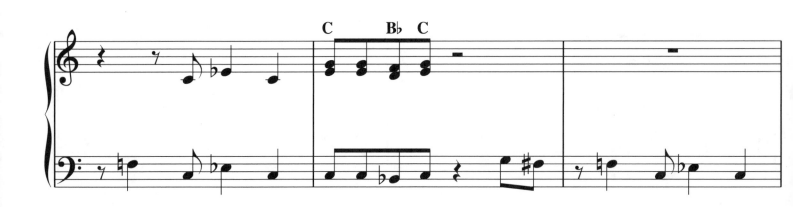

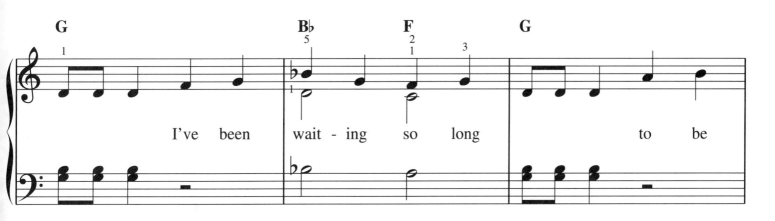

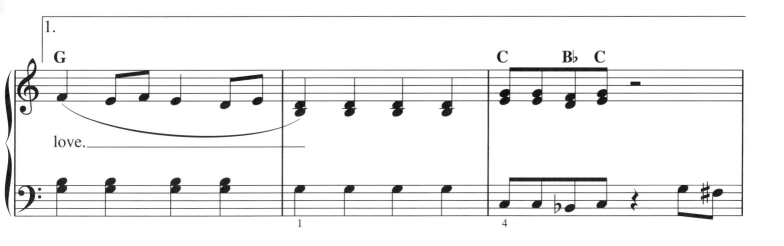

TEARS IN HEAVEN
(From The Motion Picture *RUSH*)

Words and Music by ERIC CLAPTON
and WILL JENNINGS

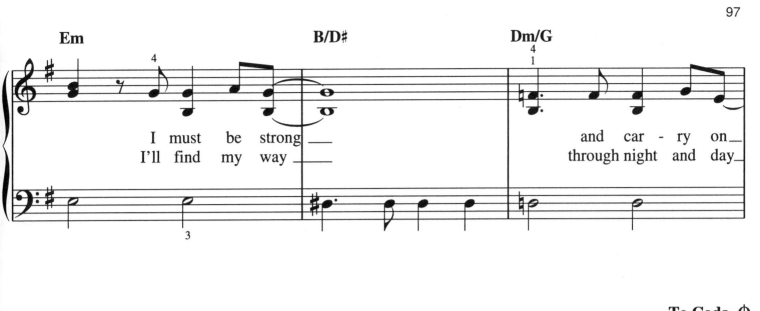

Em   **B/D♯**   **Dm/G**

I must be strong ___ and car - ry on__

I'll find my way ___ through night and day__

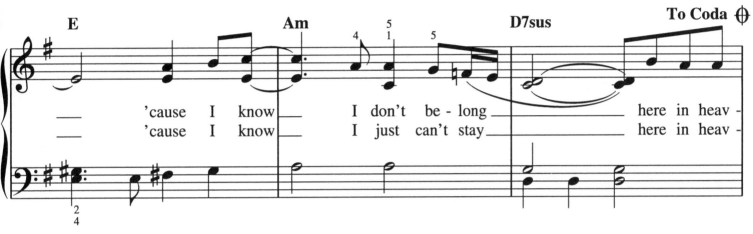

E   **Am**   **D7sus**   **To Coda**

__ 'cause I know __ I don't be - long ___ here in heav -

__ 'cause I know __ I just can't stay ___ here in heav -

G   **D/F♯**   **Em**   **G/D**   **1.** **C/E**   **D7sus**   **D7**

en.

en.

G   **2.** **C/E**   **D7sus**   **D7**   **G**

98

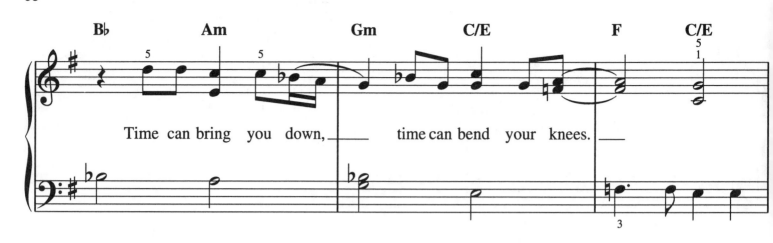

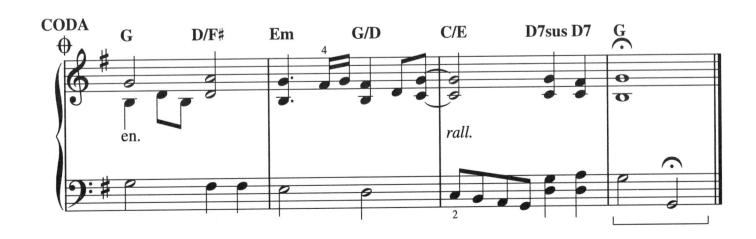

TULSA TIME

Words and Music by
DANNY FLOWERS

With a steady beat

I left Ok - la - ho - ma   driv - in' in a Pon - ti - ac
there I was in Hol - ly - wood   wish - in' I was do - in' good,

just a - bout to lose___ my   mind.   I was
talk - in' on the tel - e - phone   line.   But they don't

goin' to Ar - i - zo - na, may - be   on to Cal - i - for - nia where the
need me in the mov - ies and no - bod - y sings my songs.

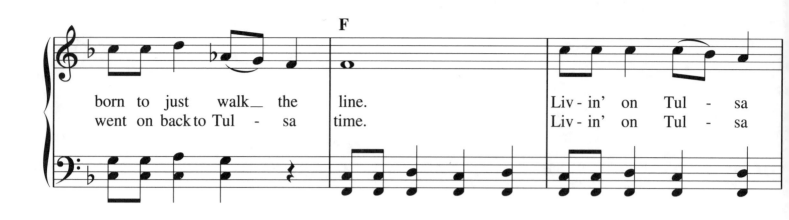

WHITE ROOM

Words and Music by JACK BRUCE
and PETE BROWN

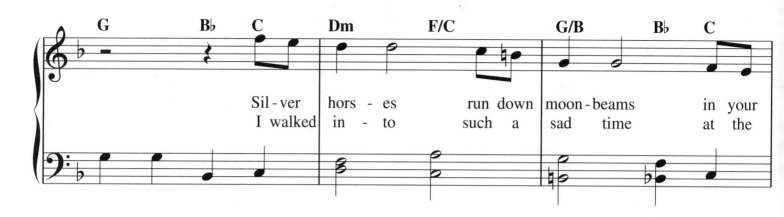

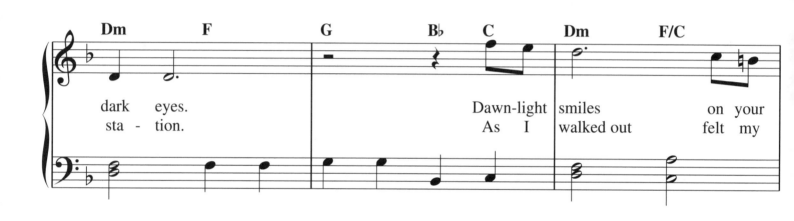

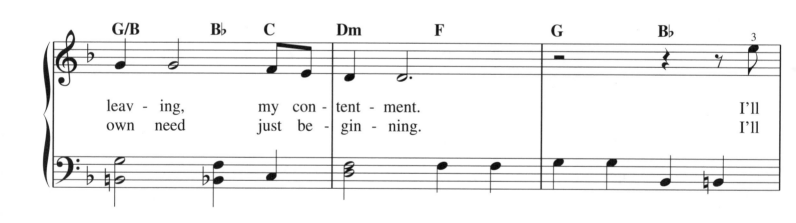

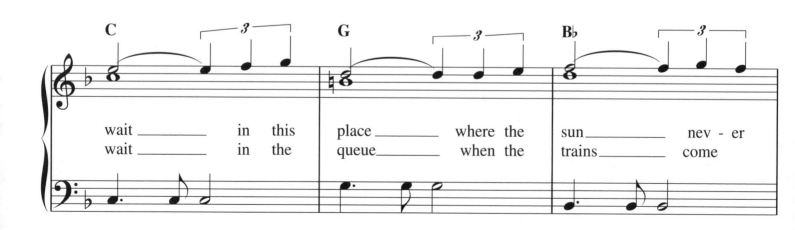

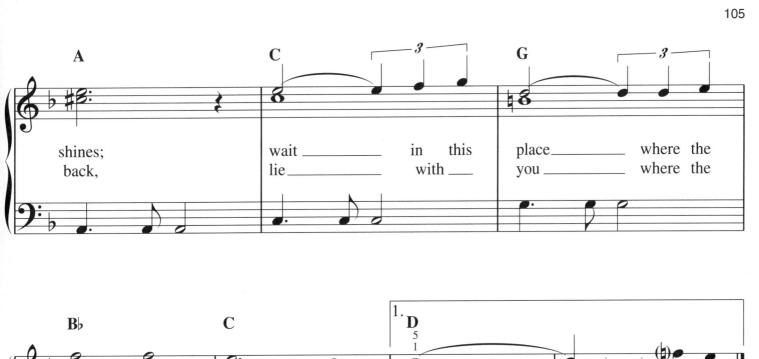

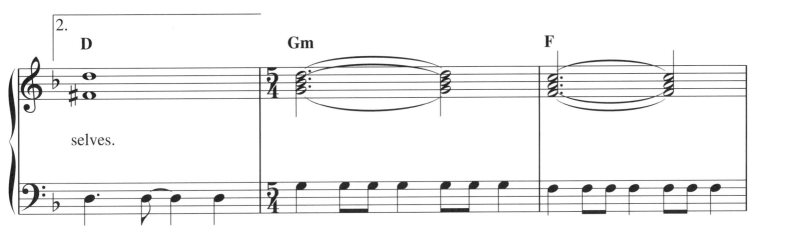

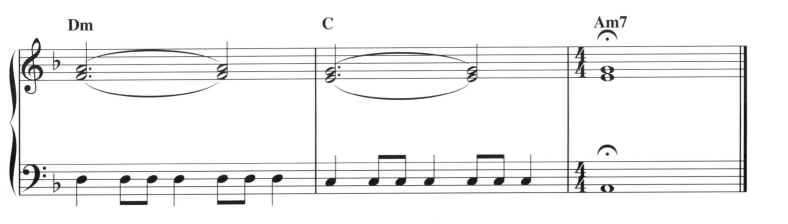

WONDERFUL TONIGHT

Words and Music by
ERIC CLAPTON

long blonde hair. ___
round with me. ___
bed. _____

And then she asks me,
And then she asks me,
And then I tell her,

"Do I look all right?"
"Do you feel all right?"
as I turn out the light,

And I say, "Yes, you look
And I say, "Yes, I feel
I say, "My darling, you are

To Coda

won - der - ful to - night."
won - der - ful to -
won - der - ful to -

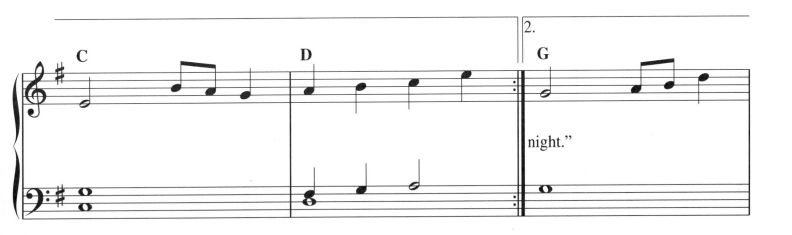

night."

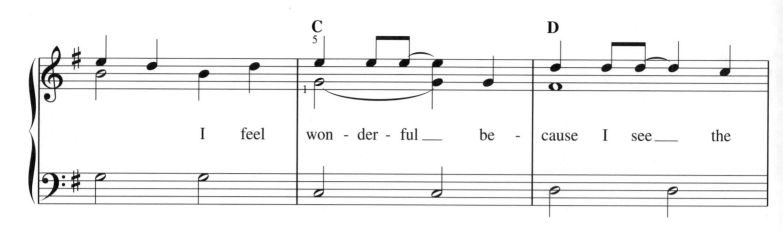

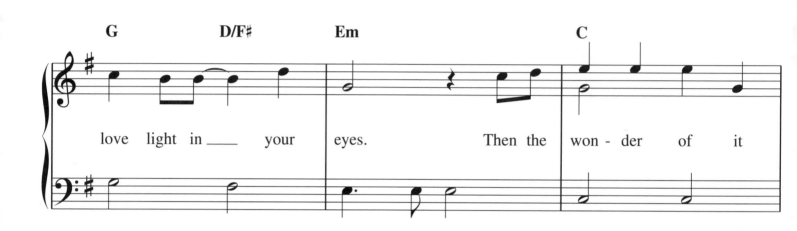

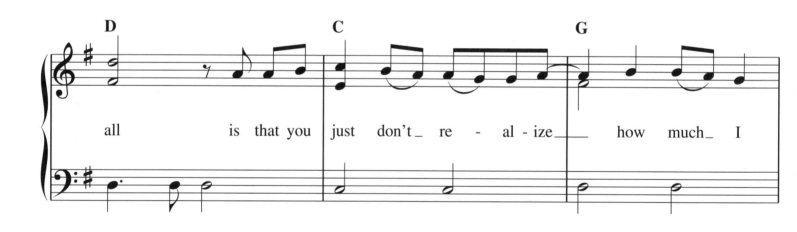

night.

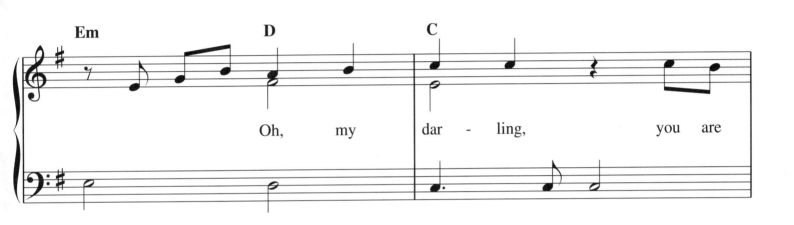

Oh, my dar - ling, you are

won - der - ful to - night."

WILLIE AND THE HAND JIVE

Words and Music by
JOHNNY OTIS

111

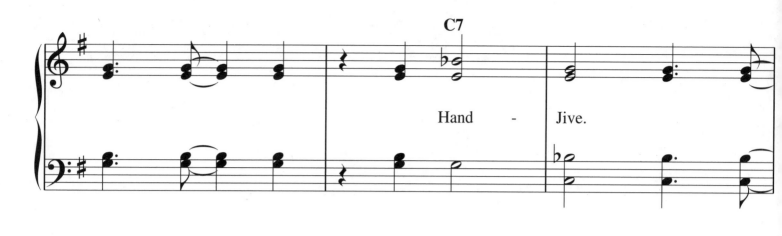

Hand - Jive.

Hand - Jive.   Hand -

Jive.   Do - in' that cra - zy Hand - Jive

5. Now.   Jive.